Anorexia and
Mimetic Desire

T0303642

Breakthroughs in Mimetic Theory

*Edited by William A. Johnsen*

# Anorexia and Mimetic Desire
René Girard

*Translated by Mark R. Anspach*

**Michigan State University Press**

East Lansing

♾ The paper used in this publication meets the minimum requirements of
ANSI/NISO Z39.48-1992 (R 1997) (Permanence of Paper).

Michigan State University Press
East Lansing, Michigan 48823-5245

Printed and bound in the United States of America.

19  18  17  16  15  14  13        1  2  3  4  5  6  7  8  9  10

Library of Congress Cataloging-in-Publication Data
Girard, Rene, 1923–
Anorexia and mimetic desire / Rene Girard ; translated by Mark R. Anspach.
pages cm. — (Breakthroughs in mimetic theory)
Includes bibliographical references.
ISBN 978-1-61186-087-0 (pbk. : alk. paper) — ISBN 978-1-60917-376-0 (ebook)
1. Anorexia nervosa. 2. Anorexia nervosa — Psychological aspects. 3. Desire (Philosophy)
4. Philosophy, French — 20th century. I. Title.
RC552.A5G57 2013
616.85′262 — dc23
2012049437

Cover and book design by Erin Kirk New.
Composition by Charlie Sharp, Sharp Designs, Lansing, Michigan
Cover art © Ali Mazraie Shadi. All rights reserved.

Michigan State University Press is a member of the Green Press Initiative and is
committed to developing and encouraging ecologically responsible publishing
practices. For more information about the Green Press Initiative and the use of
recycled paper in book publishing, please visit *www.greenpressinitiative.org*.

Visit Michigan State University Press at *www.msupress.org*

# Contents

# Foreword

*Jean-Michel Oughourlian*

*Translated by M. B. DeBevoise*

If appetite is stimulated by eating, the lack of appetite, *anorexia*, is stimulated by not eating. It is clear, then, that the natural need to eat, to feed oneself, can become mimetically overloaded and transformed first into a desire, then into a passionate desire, either to deprive oneself of food or to gorge oneself. The idea that both anorexia and bulimia are diseases of desire is what interests René Girard. For Girard, desire is mimetic, and therefore competitive: every desire springs from rivalry, every rivalry from desire.

Desire has no interest in health. Passion, when it seizes control of the mind, has still less. Eating disorders are an illuminating example of this fact. Need is subservient to desire, sometimes being deflected by it, other times perverted, even eliminated altogether.

Two opposite desires, to deprive oneself of food and to gorge oneself, can each gain possession of a person and corrupt the normal impulse to eat, leading in the one case to extreme thinness in the other to obesity. These desires, anorexia and bulimia, figure prominently in the work of two of the greatest modern artists, Alberto Giacometti and Fernando Botero. Giacometti's spindly silhouettes plainly manifest a fierce determination not to eat, whereas Botero's paintings and sculptures depict a world in which not only men and women are obese, but also cats and birds. Here, of course, art is a model to be imitated. More than this, however, it heralds and embodies two pathologies of desire that were to mark the end of the twentieth century and the beginning of the twenty-first.

The psychological preoccupation with weight loss is characterized as a nosological entity exhibiting three properties: anorexia, emaciation, and amenorrhea. Absence of menstruation is a fundamental diagnostic element, as the disorder classically—and indeed in a majority of cases—affects young girls, though more young boys are beginning to suffer from it as well. Anorexia may present itself in a simple clinical form as a refusal to eat or in a more complex form where overeating is followed by self-induced vomiting (bulimia). The desire to lose weight may also be satisfied through intensive physical exercise or the habitual use of laxatives and diuretics.

From the mimetic point of view, it is easy to see why thinness has become the feminine ideal of beauty today. Fashion models are now so skinny that they actually resemble Giacometti's sculptures; almost no celebrity or supermodel resembles one of Botero's figures. Mimetic analysis suggests that the current epidemic of anorexia is a contagion, propagating a filiform standard of beauty among adolescent girls and causing them to become obsessed with the need to lose weight in order to look like the ultra-slender goddesses of the cinema, television, and glossy magazines.

But mimetic desire also has a competitive aspect. The German-born psychiatrist Hilde Bruch intuited this competitiveness, it seems, in connecting anorexia with a sense of powerlessness and a yearning to rebel against powerlessness. She saw anorexia chiefly as a way of exerting control and of avoiding any relationship that resists such control, particularly amorous and sexual relationships. The interest of this view, I think, is that by freeing itself from psychoanalytic interpretations that posit a rejection of femininity and maternal identification it is able to regard anorexia as fundamentally a disease of rivalry, and therefore of desire.

Rivalry with whom or with what? With oneself in the first place—with one's body, one's needs, in order to achieve self-control, domination over oneself. Anorexia is therefore both a personal challenge and a form of asceticism. But it is also a rivalry with others, a struggle for power: the anorexic very quickly becomes the center of family attention and her situation a sort of Roman circus in which the rival desires of those around her—all of whom want her to eat—clash with her own desire not to eat, which holds the whole family spellbound. This phase of protracted combat eventually gives way to a medical solution. Appeal to a recognized "authority," the physician, formalizes the defeat and surrender of the anorexic's parents and introduces her to another, more formidable rival.

Anorexia therefore confers power, enabling a person who

refuses to eat to triumph over her family. In this sense, it is a kind of terrorism: the anorexic takes herself hostage and bends everyone to her will.

The question arises whether this power—so dearly acquired at the price of one's health, perhaps even of one's life—must always be purely negative. Can it ever be something other than a spasm of self-defeating antagonism, a sickness of desire that finds its sole justification in a Pyrrhic victory?

One quite remarkable example casts a new light on anorexic behavior: the famous hunger strike of Mahatma Gandhi in 1947. As violence spread throughout the Indian subcontinent, setting Muslims and Hindus against one another—when no force in the world, no thing or person, seemed able to arrest this descent into blind cruelty, to stop the massacres, to stop the burnings of mosques and temples— the Mahatma stopped eating!

As he prolonged his fast, day after day, the Mahatma grew steadily weaker. But his influence over his followers strengthened. Suddenly, the new nation was hypnotized by the Mahatma's "anorexia" and thought only of him. Day after day, the newspapers and radio reported on the deteriorating state of his health. Everyone began to fear the worst—with the result that a skeletal, comatose old man, by nothing more than an unyielding refusal to eat, managed to put an end to violence among hundreds of millions of human beings. It was not until Prime Minister Jawaharlal Nehru received the solemn undertaking of the leaders of all faiths to cease fighting, until Nehru went to the dying man's bedside and assured him that the entire country was at peace, that the Mahatma finally accepted a bowl of broth. As the Mahatma regained his strength, all of India came alive again as well.

In the apocalyptic world that René Girard has described for us, a world filled with models who are so many rivals, and with rivals who are so many models, is it beyond our imagining that young people might stop eating and risk their lives in order to put an end to the violence they see around them? An end to the competitive tensions they see in their parents' marriage, to the conflict among their siblings and among their friends, to the conflict at school and perhaps even in the world beyond—all things to which young boys, but especially young girls, are particularly sensitive?

If this view of the matter is not wrong, anorexia needs to

be seen, at least in part, as a disease of desire and of rivalry, rather than as an unmotivated form of madness. No longer associated exclusively with despair and discouragement by the medical profession, the current epidemic may one day take on a more hopeful meaning for humanity.

# Introduction: Anorexia and the Spirit of the Times

*Mark R. Anspach*

There are fashions even in the manner of suffering...

—*André Gide*

The fashion is one of weighing victims.

—*René Girard*

*Thin is in, stout is out.*[1] It was not always so. In 1911, French physician Francis Heckel wrote that his patients sometimes resisted losing weight, preferring to "stay obese for reasons of fashionable appearance." The need to have an "impressive *décolleté*" made every woman feel "duty-bound" to fatten the upper part of her body, from the neck to the breasts, which could not be done without gaining weight elsewhere.

If health reasons obliged a woman to reduce her abdomen, she would have to accept losing weight higher up. This was a "true sacrifice," emphasized Heckel, for it meant renouncing "what the world considers beautiful."[2]

A passage of the celebrated treatise on dream interpretation published a few years earlier by a Viennese psychiatrist confirms that slimness was not yet, in that era, the supreme criterion of feminine beauty. Sigmund Freud quotes a female patient's account of a dream she had about food:

> I wanted to give a supper-party, but I had nothing in the house but a little smoked salmon. I thought I would go out and buy something, but remembered then that it was Sunday afternoon and all the shops would be shut. Next I tried to ring up some caterers, but the telephone was out of order. So I had to abandon my wish to give a supper-party.[3]

In the course of the analytic session, Freud learns that the patient had just paid a visit to a woman friend whose favorite dish was salmon. The patient's husband always praised this friend, which made the patient jealous. "Fortunately," Freud noted, "this friend of hers is very skinny and thin and her husband admires a plumper figure." The patient would therefore have had little cause for worry, if the thin friend had not spoken of her desire to fatten up, inquiring: "When are you going to ask us to another meal? You always feed one so well." This statement allows Freud to explain to his patient the meaning of the dream: "It is just as though when she made this suggestion you said to yourself: 'A likely thing! I'm to ask you to come and eat in my house so that you may get stout and attract my husband still more! I'd rather never give another supper-party.'"[4]

But Freud adds that this dream also lends itself to "another and subtler interpretation." The patient wished that her friend's desire, that of becoming stout, should not be fulfilled; but in her dream, it is a desire of her own that goes unfulfilled. This indicates to Freud that the patient had put herself in her friend's place, or, in other terms, "that she had 'identified' herself with her friend."[5] Thus, while the first interpretation brings to light a rivalry between the patient and her friend, the second, "subtler" interpretation posits an identification between the two.

A rivalry between two persons who identify with each other is precisely what René Girard calls a *mimetic* rivalry. For Girard, there is nothing strange about discovering an identification between rivals. On the contrary, the more one individual puts him or herself in the place of another and imitates that person, the more likely it is that competition will develop, especially if the imitation extends to the realm of desire: two persons who desire the same thing—for instance, a plump figure to please men—are apt to become rivals.

Girard explains anorexia as the extreme result of an analogous mimetic rivalry playing itself out, not between two persons only but on the scale of an entire society. In this way, Girard sets himself squarely against all interpretations, psychoanalytic or otherwise, that locate the source of the problem in the unconscious of the individual—for example, the theories that invoke "a refusal of normal sexuality." Why seek some hidden motive behind the anorexic's desire to lose weight, Girard asks, when the truth is that we *all* want to lose weight? Far from being buried deep in the mind of the patient, the real motive is clearly visible in the spirit of the times. One need only turn on the television or leaf through a women's magazine in order to appreciate the eminently mimetic character of the wish to be thin. Girard sees the rise of anorexia as spectacular proof that imitation constitutes an increasingly irresistible force in contemporary life.

Today, this same force would make Freud's plump patient covet her friend's skinnier physique, not necessarily because it would be more attractive to men—there are still husbands who prefer womanly curves—but because it would better conform to a cultural ideal of feminine beauty.

In fact, even if the desire to be sexually attractive is present at the start, mimetic rivalries tend to acquire a life of their own. When such rivalries intensify beyond a certain threshold, the original objective fades from view until all that remains is the desire to outdo one's adversary. In the case of anorexia, that means being the skinniest, whatever the cost. Of course, since men are mimetic too, they may well desire thin women—not because they find them intrinsically more attractive, but because they look more like the models of desirable women offered up by movies, television, and advertising.

These models define the standard against which other

women are measured. But the standard is not stable, because the women who serve as models are in competition among themselves. For Girard, it is the very dynamic of rivalry that keeps driving the movement forward. Since actresses and fashion models constantly strive to surpass one another, they must become thinner and thinner, leaving ordinary women feeling fatter and fatter. In 1995, when Girard first gave the lecture printed here, one-third of American high school girls saw themselves as overweight; a dozen years later, the figure had soared to a whopping 90 percent.[6]

Mimetic rivalries are characterized by a tendency to escalation. This tendency may be seen in the words that Freud puts in the mouth of the patient reluctant to cook for the friend who wanted to get fatter: *I'd rather never give another supper!* Anorexics practice a similar escalation in their desire not to get fatter. What they say, in effect, is: *I'd rather never go to another supper!* In a classic work originally published in 1963, Mara Selvini Palazzoli observes that all of her patients avoid eating with others: "They abhor the family table," preferring "to eat alone, on their feet, in their room or the kitchen, without setting the table, in a haphazard, improvised manner."[7] As Girard remarks, such habits have become typical of the times. But true anorexics eat so little that they become dangerously emaciated, claiming all the while not to be hungry.

*Anorexia* literally means "lack of appetite."[8] Girard rightly emphasizes that the term is misleading. As the authors of the monograph *Anorexia Nervosa* noted, appetite may be absent, but it may also be present in a distorted form or even increased. Some patients, the authors state,

> have a true anorexia and genuinely have no desire
> for food. Others crave food but refuse to eat. Some
> eat and then vomit; whereas others surreptitiously
> hide or dispose of their meals so as not to arouse
> the suspicion and disapproval of their families and
> physician. There are those who fear to eat because
> digestion may cause fearful somatic distress or lead
> to obesity and there are a few who eat docilely and
> then purge themselves of the offensive nutriments
> by cathartics and enemas. But in every case,
> although the reasons and strategems will vary, the

final result is a reduction in the intake of calories, a loss of weight and semi-starvation.[9]

Selvini Palazzoli emphasizes the role of weight loss in anorexia, suggesting that the essence of the pathology is better captured by the German term *Pubertätsmagersucht,* meaning a "pubescent quest for thinness"—or, as she describes it, a *mania* for thinness.[10] Other leading specialists take the same approach when defining the term: Hilde Bruch views anorexia as distinguished by "a relentless pursuit of thinness," and G. F. M. Russell defines it as "a morbid fear of being fat."[11]

Anorexics invariably claim they were "too fat" at the time they started dieting. Most often, they were not truly obese but simply dismayed to find themselves filling out or becoming a bit plump in adolescence. Bruch recalls a typical case going back to the era when anorexia was first recognized as an illness by modern medicine. In 1868, a 15-year-old girl, described as short but with a pleasing figure, began "looking with envy upon her slim friends and complaining about her 'exaggerated embonpoint.'" A year later, embarrassed to have put on more weight, she went on a diet and completely transformed her appearance, becoming frail, pallid, and wrinkled after only eight months.[12]

Referring to her own patients, Bruch observes that nothing about their initial decision to go on a diet seems any different "from that of countless adolescents who watch their weight in our slimness-conscious society." As Girard stresses, a mania for thinness is part of the spirit of the times. The difference between these girls and their peers becomes apparent only later, when a diet "explicitly undertaken with the intent of becoming more attractive and more respected does not lead to better relationships as the weight drops, but results in increasing social withdrawal and often extreme isolation."[13] To reformulate this observation in Girardian terms: the original objective falls by the wayside in those cases where the competitive desire to be the skinniest wins out over everything else.

As we noted earlier, mimetic rivalries have a tendency to escalate. This tendency is particularly visible in warfare, which is characterized by what Girard, in his rereading of Carl von Clausewitz, calls an "escalation to extremes."[14] The anorexic phenomenon displays an escalation to extremes of a more discreet and enigmatic variety. The escalation of violence that causes men to kill each other on the battlefield is easier to understand than the escalation of dieting that leads women to die of starvation. What could be more compelling than the need to eat? Can the mimetic impulse overcome the most elemental of appetites and force the body to fit the mold it imposes?

Since Girard first developed his mimetic interpretation of eating disorders, a growing number of scientific studies have highlighted the way models in the media contribute to the problem. In a survey of American girls, for example, 69 percent of respondents said that pictures of women in magazines influenced their idea of the perfect body, and 47 percent affirmed that they wanted to lose weight because of those pictures; the total proportion of participants who wanted to become thinner (66 percent) was more than twice the number who were actually overweight (29 percent).[15] A laboratory experiment in England directly tested the influence exercised by photographs of women in fashion magazines on anorexic or bulimic patients. After the patients spent only six or seven minutes looking at such photos, their overestimation of their own body size rose by 25 percent.[16]

The powerful impact of televised images was dramatically verified in a corner of the Fiji Islands where televisions were not available before 1995. In the past, it was rare to find natives who dieted, because traditional Fijian culture views a strong appetite and a robust body in a positive light. Yet only three years after the arrival of the first televisions, 74 percent of surveyed high school girls reported feeling "too fat" at least part of the time, and 69 percent had already made an attempt at dieting to lose weight. But the most astounding finding of the study was that 11 percent had resorted to self-inflicted vomiting, compared with 0 percent in 1995. In the course of interviews, the girls confirmed that television personalities had become models for them. One girl expressed a desire to be "taller and thinner" like Cindy Crawford; another spoke of her friends wanting to resemble the rich California students depicted on *Beverly Hills 90210*. Still another said, "I want to imitate [the stars of the Australian series *Shortland Street*]—the way they live, the type of food they eat."[17] Is this Fijian teenager so different from the anorexic patient of

Bruch's who "observed slim women or tall boys . . . and would imitate what they ate"?[18]

Certain anorexics push their identification with others even further. Bruch records the extreme case of an 18-year-old patient who managed to satisfy her own appetite vicariously through her tablemates, as if she put herself directly in their place. This patient "would assume the identity of whomever she was around, and by watching others eat, in a way, 'have people eat for her,' and feel 'full' after that, without having eaten at all." After a period of fasting, the same girl explained: "I keep my mind eternally preoccupied with what size I am, always hoping it will become smaller. If I must eat—that takes too much mental energy to decide what, how much, and why must I. Every day I wake up in prison, actually enjoying the confinement."[19]

It is difficult here not to think of the Franz Kafka short story that Girard cites, "A Hunger Artist." Kafka's protagonist—having chosen to be exhibited as a fasting champion after failing to find any nourishment to his liking—is literally imprisoned in a cage without food. To guarantee that he does not cheat by eating on the sly, men are posted by the cage to watch him all night, and "his happiest moment was when the morning came and an enormous breakfast was brought them, at his expense"[20]—exactly as if he relied on them to eat for him.

Selvini Palazzoli's patients often express their great interest in food through "the hobby of cooking 'for others,' even during the illness, elaborate dishes and desserts."[21] This apparent solicitude may conceal a less admirable ulterior motive. In a game where the biggest loser of weight is the winner, whoever consents to gain weight will lose. Encouraging others to eat gives the anorexic an added advantage in the race to be thin. It is just as though she said to herself: *I'd rather never go to supper again—but I'm happy to cook for you so that you will eat heartily and get fat!* As in the potlatch ritual that Girard discusses in the text published here, conspicuous non-consumption goes hand in hand with the urge to make others consume.

To refrain from eating while others eat is to claim for oneself the coveted position of the *victim*, and the competition to be the greatest victim can have tragic consequences. At the end of Kafka's story, the fasting champion dies of starvation.

But the modern concern for victims, which makes the ritualized sacrifice of scapegoats impossible, endows victimhood with so much prestige that it turns into an object of rivalry itself. Violent impulses that no longer have a ritual outlet are now channeled into a veritable *competition of victims,* triggering a sacrificial escalation in the contest to see who can boast of having suffered the most. As Girard has remarked elsewhere, "the fashion is one of weighing victims."[22] In the case of anorexia, the metaphor must be taken literally. The victim who weighs the least carries the most weight; she walks off with the trophy.

Like the mania for thinness, victim competition is part of the spirit of the times. This observation may help us understand the current rise in anorexia, but it does not explain why the most severe form of the pathology strikes certain girls in particular. All young women are exposed to the spirit of the times, yet only a few take the weight-loss game to dangerous extremes. What makes some more determined than the rest to be the biggest losers? In the text published here and the accompanying interview, René Girard downplays the importance of the family environment and places greater emphasis on the social context. However justified this approach may be, the therapist has no choice but to work with individual patients and their families. The question necessarily arises as to whether there is anything particular that characterizes these families.

Selvini Palazzoli provides a striking answer to this question. In the families that she treated, she repeatedly observed the same distinctive type of interaction within the parental couple, namely a *rivalry for the victim's role.* Each partner played the martyr, attempting to make the other feel guilty. Each posed as the one making generous sacrifices for the good of the family. The mothers defended this self-representation by openly trying to induce guilt in anyone who questioned it, while the fathers, "retreating into a gloomy silence, would blame everyone for the unfairness and incomprehension of which they felt themselves to be the victims." This kind of interaction leads to a perverse game of one-upmanship in which the biggest loser wins:

> Two moralistic spouses who both feel themselves
> to be the victims of a compulsive relationship are
> bound to compete for the most coveted moral

trophy: which of them is the bigger victim. The reciprocal positioning in the relationship is thus of the symmetrical type, but it is a very peculiar symmetry: the upper hand belongs to the one who has a greater feeling of being sacrificed—to duty, propriety, and the stability of the family as an institution. We therefore resolved to define this type of symmetry as being characterized by a *sacrificial escalation*.[23]

This paradoxical game puts the patient into an uncomfortable position with her parents. Each of them wants to capture the daughter's sympathy; but if she should approach either too closely, she will immediately be pushed away, because winning her sympathy would undermine the status of victim to which the parent is attached.[24]

Selvini Palazzoli suggests that in a family system where every attempt at communication is liable to be refused, the refusal of food might constitute a logical response.[25] What we would like to underscore, however, is the remarkable correspondence that exists between her description of the family context and Girard's observations about the social context. This correspondence makes it possible to connect the two levels of analysis.

A girl raised in a home environment marked by sacrificial competition is more likely to throw herself into the sacrificial competition at the social level that pushes women to renounce eating properly. Fortunately, the victims who lose their life trying to win this competition are still relatively few in number. But the exceptional nature of their fate should not keep us from recognizing how much they have in common with their peers. Imitating the same cultural model that other women imitate—imitating all those who imitate that model—and taking the imitation as far as possible is what leads these women to sacrifice themselves on the altar of thinness. They die as a result of identifying with other women too much.

One may apply to these victims a comment that Freud, in the text cited earlier, makes about the type of identification he observed between his patient and her friend. Such identification, he says, "enables patients to express in their symptoms not only their own experiences but those of a large number of other people; it enables them, as it were, to suffer on behalf of a whole crowd of people . . ."[26] And so it is that, starting out from a mimetic rivalry, we arrive at the martyrdom of a victim who suffers in the place of a crowd. If the mania for thinness belongs to the spirit of the times, hasn't the mechanism it triggers been with us since the foundation of the world?

## Acknowledgments

The author of this introduction wishes to thank the psychotherapists Françoise Domenach, of the Institut d'études systémiques in Paris, and Matteo Selvini, of the Centri Mara Selvini Anoressia e Disturbi alimentari in Milan, for having read the manuscript of his text. He would also like to extend his appreciation to Peter Thiel, Robert Hamerton-Kelly and Imitatio for the support accorded his work. He is alone responsible for the ideas expressed.

# Notes

1. See Hugh Klein and K. S. Shiffman, "Thin is 'in' and stout is 'out': what animated cartoons tell viewers about body weight," *Eating and Weight Disorders* 10 (June 2005): 107–16. This study demonstrates that, even in cartoons, the number of thin characters, especially female ones, continued to rise from the 1930s to the 1990s.

2. Francis Heckel, *Les Grandes et Petites Obésités* (Paris: Masson, 1911); quoted in Hilde Bruch, *Eating Disorders: Obesity, Anorexia Nervosa, and the Person Within* (London: Routledge & Kegan Paul, 1974), 18–19.

3. Sigmund Freud, *The Interpretation of Dreams,* trans. James Strachey (New York: Avon, 1965), 180. We thank Dr. Henri Grivois for drawing our attention to the relevance this passage might have in the context of a discussion of anorexia.

4. Freud, *Interpretation of Dreams,* 181–82.

5. Freud, *Interpretation of Dreams,* 182.

6. Holly Brubach, "Starved to Perfection," *New York Times,* April 15, 2007.

7. Mara Selvini Palazzoli, *L'anoressia mentale: Dalla terapia individuale alla terapia familiare,* revised edition (Milan: Raffaello Cortina, 2006), 23.

8. The term was used to designate the modern clinical entity in 1873 by Lasègue, who spoke of "hysterical anorexia," followed closely by Gull, who, after having initially referred to "hysterical apepsia," coined the expression *anorexia nervosa* still employed today in English-speaking countries. In 1883, Huchard proposed the appellation "anorexie mentale," which was adopted in France and Italy.

9. Eugene L. Bliss and C. H. Hardin Branch, *Anorexia Nervosa* (New York: Hoeber, 1960); quoted in Selvini Palazzoli, *L'anoressia mentale,* 27.

10. Selvini Palazzoli, *L'anoressia mentale,* 25.

11. Both formulations are cited by Bruch, *Eating Disorders,* 223–24.

12. Bruch, *Eating Disorders,* 212, 258.

13. Bruch, *Eating Disorders,* 255, 258.

14. See René Girard, *Battling to the End: Conversations with Benoît Chantre*, trans. Mary Baker (East Lansing: Michigan State University Press, 2010).

15. A. E. Field et al., "Exposure to the Mass Media and Weight Concerns Among Girls," *Pediatrics* 103, no. 3 (March 1999).

16. Kate Hamilton and Glen Waller, "Media Influences on Body Size Estimation in Anorexia and Bulimia: An Experimental Study," *British Journal of Psychiatry* 162 (1993): 839.

17. A. E. Becker et al., "Eating Behaviours and Attitudes Following Prolonged Exposure to Television among Ethnic Fijian Adolescent Girls," *British Journal of Psychiatry* 180 (2002): 509–11, 513.

18. Bruch, *Eating Disorders,* 93.

19. Bruch, *Eating Disorders,* 93.

20. Franz Kafka, "A Hunger Artist," in *The Penal Colony: Stories and Short Pieces,* trans. Willa and Edwin Muir (New York: Schocken, 1961), 245.

21. Selvini Palazzoli, *L'anoressia mentale,* 26.

22. René Girard, *I See Satan Fall Like Lightning,* trans. James G. Williams (Maryknoll, N.Y.: Orbis, 2001), 166.

23. Selvini Palazzoli, *L'anoressia mentale,* 220 (emphasis added).

24. Selvini Palazzoli, *L'anoressia mentale,* 221.

25. Selvini Palazzoli, *L'anoressia mentale,* 222.

26. Freud, *The Interpretation of Dreams,* 183. Freud is speaking here of what he calls "hysterical identification," which he defines as "not simple imitation but *assimilation* [of a symptom] on the basis of a similar ætiological pretension." Hysteria may be regarded as the feminine pathology in vogue at that time. Let us recall that Lasègue and Gull had initially described anorexia as a hysterical illness.

# Eating Disorders
# and Mimetic Desire

*René Girard*

Among younger women, eating disorders are reaching epidemic proportions. The most widespread and spectacular
at this moment is the most recently identified, the so-called
bulimia nervosa, characterized by binge eating followed by
"purging," sometimes through laxatives or diuretics, more
often through self-induced vomiting. Some researchers claim
that in American colleges at least one third of the female
student population is involved to some degree. (Since nine
out of ten sufferers are women I will use feminine pronouns
in this paper, but some undergraduates at Stanford tell me
that the epidemic is spreading to male students.)

G.M.F. Russell, the first researcher who focused on the
specific aspects of modern bulimia, is usually presented as the
discoverer of a new illness. The title of his 1979 publication

contradicts this view: "Bulimia Nervosa: An Ominous Variant of Anorexia Nervosa." And, indeed, all the symptoms he describes had been mentioned before in connection with anorexia (see Bruch).

The insurance companies and the medical profession like only well-defined illnesses, and so does the public. We all try to distance ourselves from pathological contamination by giving it a name. Eating disorders are often discussed as if they were new varieties of measles or of typhoid fever.

Why distrust the distinction between two illnesses with symptoms as radically opposed as those of anorexia and bulimia? Because we live in a world where eating too much and not eating enough are opposite but inseparable ways of coping with the slenderness imperative that dominates our collective imaginations. Most of us oscillate all our lives between attenuated forms of these two pathologies.

The layperson understands perfectly a truth that most specialists prefer not to confront. Our eating disorders are caused by our compulsive desire to lose weight. Most books on the subject acknowledge the universal calorie phobia but somewhat absent-mindedly, as if it could not be the major cause of a serious illness. How could a fundamentally healthy desire become the cause of pathological behavior, even of death?

Many people would be healthier, no doubt, if they ate less. In view of this fact, it is not illogical to suppose that, in anorexia, there must be some motivation other than this healthy desire, some unconscious drive, no doubt, that generates abnormal behavior. By turning anorexia and bulimia into two separate pathologies, the classifiers make it easier for us to lose sight of their common basis.

## The Bankruptcy of Modern Theories

The search for hidden motivations is the alpha and omega, of course, of our modern culture. Our number one principle is that no human phenomenon is really what it seems to be. A satisfactory interpretation must rely on one of the hermeneutics of suspicion that have become popular in the nineteenth and twentieth century, or on several of these, on a cocktail of *soupçon:* psychoanalysis, Marxism, feminism, etc.

We automatically assume that social phenomena have little if anything to do with what is obvious in them, in this case the rejection of food.

In anorexia, psychoanalysts usually diagnose "a refusal of normal sexuality," due to the patient's excessive desire "to please her father," etc. These explanations are still invoked in books being written right now but the voice is growing fainter. Around this sort of thing the smell of mustiness is overpowering. Even in Lacan's own land, the old arrogance is gone.

Early in my life, I had an opportunity to observe that the eating practices of young women have nothing to do with a desire to please their fathers. Just before World War II, a pretty cousin of mine was dieting furiously, and her father, my uncle, was storming about helplessly, trying to get her to eat more. Fathers, as a rule, are not pleased to see their daughters starve themselves. This particular father was also a physician, at a time when the medical profession had not yet caught the disease it was already trying to cure.

This uncle was our family doctor and, as such, had great prestige in my eyes, at least until that day. I had not yet read Freud but my later skepticism regarding his conception of fatherhood may well originate in this incident. I immediately perceived that my cousin was listening to a command more powerful than her father's desire and, with the passing of time, this more authoritative voice has become louder and louder. It emanates from the people who really count in our adolescence and who are our peers and contemporaries rather than our fathers. The individual models of young people reinforce the authority of the collective models which are the media, Hollywood, and television. The message is always the same: we have to get thinner, regardless of the cost.

The compulsive dieters *really* want to be thin, and most of us are secretly aware of this because most of us also want to be thin. All our convoluted systems of explanation, based on sexuality, social class, power, the tyranny of male over female, and *tutti quanti* are floundering on this ridiculous but irrefutable fact. The capitalist system is no more responsible for this situation than fathers are, or the male gender as a whole.

The capitalist system is clever enough, no doubt, to adjust to the rage for thinness and it invents all sorts of products supposedly capable of helping us in our battle against calories, but its own instinct runs the other way. It systematically favors consumption over abstinence, and it certainly did not invent our dieting hysteria.

It is the intellectual beauty of our eating disorders at this point in our history that they make manifest the bankruptcy of all the theories that continue to dominate our universities. The problem is not that these eating disorders are too complex for our current systems of interpretation—which would make our explicators salivate with delight. The problem is that they are too simple, too readily intelligible.

## The Need for Common Sense

All we need, to understand the symptoms described by the specialists, is to observe our own behavior with food. At some time or other, most of us experience at least an attenuated version of the various symptoms that characterize our two main eating disorders. When things are not going well, we tend to take refuge in some form of excess, which turns into a quasi-addiction.

Since food is still the least dangerous drug, most of us resort to a mild form of bulimia. When the situation improves, we revive our New Year resolutions and we go on a strict diet. Feeling in control once again, we experience a psychological lift not unlike the exhilaration of the true anorexic.

Between these "normal" oscillations on the one hand, and bulimia and anorexia on the other hand, the distance is great, no doubt, but the path is unbroken. We all have the same goal, to lose weight, and, to some of us, this goal is so important that the means to reach it no longer matter. *Qui veut la fin veut les moyens.* The anorexic pattern of behavior makes sense within the context not of our nominal values but of what we silently teach our children when we stop chattering about values.

Both the anorexic and the bulimic manage to reduce their calorie intake to a level that will reach or exceed the degree of thinness generally regarded as desirable at any given time. The true anorexic is able to reach this goal directly, simply by refraining from eating. The bulimic reaches this goal indirectly by eating as much as she pleases and then by vomiting much of the food she absorbs. In the competition for absolute thinness, the true anorexic is Julius Caesar, Alexander the Great, and Napoleon all rolled into one. In quite a few cases, she does so well that she literally starves herself to death.

Contrary to what the etymology of the word deceptively suggests, the anorexic has an appetite. She still wants to eat just as much as we do and much more, because she is hungrier than we are. Some anorexic patients fear that if they ate a single bite, they would never stop eating. In other words they would become bulimic. And this is, indeed, what occasionally happens. That is why these people never relax. Through superhuman effort, they have triumphed over their normal instinct, and now the spirit of unnatural thinness possesses them so completely that the notion of demonic possession suits their case better than the vocabulary of modern psychiatry. The food they formerly craved becomes truly repugnant. Every time their doctor or some well-meaning relative tricks them into absorbing some nourishment, they feel nauseated. They know that, in a single instant, they may lose everything they worked so hard to acquire. Their love-hate relationship to food is understandable. Their tremendous energy in everything they undertake fulfills a dual purpose: it takes their mind away from the desire to eat and it helps them lose more weight.

Anorexia strikes the best and the brightest among our young women. The typical victim is well educated, talented, ambitious, eager for perfection. She is the super-achiever type and she knows she is playing by the rules suggested by the most powerful voices in our culture, including the medical profession. Researchers at the Harvard medical school have recently "discovered" that the weight formerly regarded as ideal for women is too high by twenty-five per cent and the lowering of it would give women "a much better chance of survival."

The anorexic is too loyal a citizen of our crazy world to suspect that, as she listens to the unanimous spirit of weight reduction, she is being pushed towards self-destruction. No one can convince her that she is really ill. She interprets all attempts to help her as envious conspiracies of people who would like to cheat her out of her painfully acquired victory, being unable to match it. She is proud to fulfill what is perhaps the one and only ideal still common to our entire society, slenderness.

Many women would like to be anorexics but, fortunately, very few succeed. Even though genuine anorexia is statistically as much on the rise as the other eating disorders, it remains rare in absolute numbers. Success is so difficult to achieve that the failures are countless. The bulimics are would-be anorexics who, despairing of ever making it, go all the way to the other extreme. And then, through artificial means, they manage to cancel out the effects of their constantly repeated defeats. Which explains why, in the vomiting type of bulimia, the prognosis is better than in true anorexia.

The vomiting bulimic is still a winner of sorts. As a matter of fact, unlike the true anorexic, she can be just as thin as fashion demands and no more. In the first stages of her illness, when the physical consequences of her eating practices have not materialized, she may feel as satisfied with herself as her anorexic sister. She can eat her cake and yet not have it in her stomach long enough to assimilate the hated calories. Ultimately, her health deteriorates and she pays dearly for her binges—but not in respect to what matters most to her. She never becomes overweight.

Exercising

Given the topsy-turvy relationship of our culture to food, it is not the rise in eating disorders which is astonishing but the fact, rather, that so many people eat more or less normally. Contrary to what our nihilists and relativists tell us, there is a human nature, and its resiliency is such that it often manages to adjust to the weirdest cultural insanities.

In order to cope with the thinness imperative without getting involved in practices that endanger their health or destroy their self-respect, many people have a secret weapon: *they exercise.* Much of their time is spent walking, running, jogging, bicycling, swimming, jumping, climbing mountains, and practicing other horribly boring and strenuous activities for the sole purpose of eliminating unwanted calories.

The irritating aspect of exercise is its politically correct justification in terms of outdoor living, communion with nature, the earth mother, Thoreau, Rousseau, ecology, healthy living, the plight of victims, and the other usual excuses. The only real motivation is the desire to lose weight.

A few months ago, *The Stanford Daily* published the

statement of some resident psychiatrist, I believe, asserting that quite a few female students make an excessive and compulsive use of gymnastic facilities. In the near future, I suppose, this person will be officially credited with the discovery of an entirely new syndrome, *gymnastica nervosa* perhaps, or *jogging bulimia* ...

Don't we need a special label, as well, for these fattish professors who drag themselves up the Stanford hills carrying one heavy weight in each hand? They obviously believe that the more excruciating their ordeal, the more profitable it will be in terms of personal rejuvenation. With perspiration streaming down their faces, blinding their wildly imploring eyes, they evoke the more exotic tortures in Dante's *Inferno*. Being tenured, they could spend their lives comfortably and securely. The spectacle they offer makes one wonder if the poet's description of hell is as outrageous after all as claimed by our humanists. If they, themselves, voluntarily recreate the worst aspects of hell in their leisure time, with no outside compulsion, they unwittingly demonstrate the realism they imprudently question.

What am I doing myself on these Stanford hills? ... Is that

your question? It has no relevance to our topic and deserves no answer. I will point out, though, that no one has ever seen me carrying anything in my hands for the purpose of making myself heavier than I am.

We live at a time when the healthiest and the unhealthiest actions can have the same motivation. The true reason why many young people, especially women, join the ranks of smokers, these days, or do not give up smoking, not even at the urging of their Government, is the fear of gaining weight, a fear which this same Government, curiously, does its best to foster and intensify.

## The Mimetic Nature of Modern Eating Disorders

What is the cause of all this? As I already observed, we can no longer blame the favorite institutional scapegoats beaten to death by our master thinkers of the last two centuries. These beasts of burden have all collapsed long ago, just like Nietzsche's famous horse in Turin. One can go on beating dead horses for several decades, no doubt, especially in graduate seminars but, even there, there will be an end. No one can really believe that our families, the class system, the male gender as a whole, the Christian churches, or even a repressive university administration, might be responsible for what is going on.

Sooner or later, we must finally identify the fierce and lively obstacle that modern and postmodern theories never anticipate, the uninvited guest that no one ever expects, the mimetic rival. As long as they are respected, the hated prohibitions keep this living *commendatore* out of sight. They make mimetic rivalry more difficult, if not impossible.

Both modernism and postmodernism are helpless when confronted with the intensification of mimetic rivalry that necessarily accompanies the dissolving of all prohibitions. Like those insects that go on building their nests when their eggs are gone, our modernists and postmodernist teachers will keep blaming the dead prohibitions until doomsday, but their students, some day, should finally question this dogma.

A few years ago, a popular formula of our contemporary individualism was: looking out for number one. If we were happy with ourselves, we should not have to look out for anything, we should not always be on the lookout. When we look around, most of us discover that, far from being number one, we are lost in the crowd. In everything that matters to us, there is always someone who seems superior, in looks, in intelligence, in wealth, and most dreadful of all these days, in slenderness. Even a radical shift from the deconstructors to the Eastern mystics will not give us the peace we are looking for. Westerners are always forced into action, and when they no longer imitate heroes and saints they are drawn into the infernal circle of mimetic futility. Even at that level, especially at that level, the number one status can be achieved only through hard work and cutthroat competition.

The people with eating disorders are not the people with a religious hang-up, the traditionalists and the fundamentalists, but the most "liberated." I remember one of the *Seinfeld* shows on NBC that brilliantly captured the "normality" of bulimia nervosa in our world. At the end of a meal in New York restaurant, a young woman goes to the bathroom to vomit the large plate of spaghetti she has just finished eating. She announces this to her companion, another woman, in the same tranquil and matter-of-fact tone as, in by-gone days, she might have said: "I'll put on some lipstick."

She behaves like those decadent Romans whose stories horrified my innocent youth but she needs no slaves to tickle her throat. A good and self-reliant American woman can take care of everything all by herself. This one plays both the master and the slave in such an efficient and matter-of-fact way that it all seems perfectly natural and legitimate. She's bought this spaghetti with her own money, and she can do with it whatever she pleases. We feel that everything in her life, from her professional career to her love affairs, must be managed in the same efficient way. Watching that show, I marveled once again at the superiority of dramatic expression that can suggest in a flash what volumes of pompous "research" will never come close to apprehending.

Compared to the young woman on NBC, the decadent Romans were innocent sensualists. They, too, were eating and vomiting in turn, but for themselves only and not for anybody else. They were really looking out for number one. Our modern bulimic is eating for herself, to be sure, but she is vomiting for others, for all these women who are watching each other's waistlines. Her radical freedom is synonymous with her enslavement to the opinion of others.

Mimetic desire aims at the absolute slenderness of the radiant being some other person always is in our eyes but we ourselves never are, at least in our own eyes. To understand desire is to understand that its self-centeredness is undistinguishable from its other-centeredness.

The stoics tell me that we should take refuge in ourselves, but our bulimic selves are uninhabitable, and that is what Augustine and Pascal discovered long ago. As long as we are not provided with a goal worthy of our emptiness we will copy the emptiness of others and constantly regenerate the hell from which we are trying to escape.

Puritanical and tyrannical as our ancestors may have been, their religious and ethical principles could be disregarded with impunity, and indeed they were and we can see the result. We are really on our own. The gods we give ourselves are self-generated in the sense that they depend entirely on our mimetic desire. We thus re-invent masters more ferocious than the God of the most Jansenist Christianity. As soon as we violate the thinness imperative, we suffer all the tortures of hell and we find ourselves under a redoubled obligation to fast. Our sins are inscribed in our flesh and we must expiate them down to the last calorie, through a deprivation more severe than any religion has ever imposed upon its adepts.

Even before the thinness imperative appeared in our world, Dostoevsky realized that the new, liberated man would generate cruel forms of asceticism rooted in nihilism. The hero of *Raw Youth* fasts in order to demonstrate to himself his will to power. Even earlier, Stendhal, even though hostile to religion, had detected the same tendency in post-revolutionary French culture. The hero of *The Red and the Black* (1830) refrains from eating in order to demonstrate that he can be Napoleon.

There is great irony in the fact that the modern process of stamping out religion produces countless caricatures of it. We are often told that our problems are due to our inability to shake off our religious tradition, but this is not true. They are rooted in the debacle of that tradition, which is necessarily followed by the reappearance in modern garb of more ancient and ferocious divinities rooted in the mimetic process.

Our eating disorders are not continuous with our religion. They originate in the neopaganism of our time, in the cult of the body, in the Dionysiac mystique of Nietzsche, the first of our great dieters, by the way. They are caused by the destruction of the family and other safeguards against the forces of mimetic fragmentation and competition, unleashed by the end of prohibitions. These forces could recreate unanimity only through collective scapegoating, which cannot really occur, fortunately, in our world, because our notion of the human person, even degraded into radical individualism, prevents the reestablishment of a community founded on unanimous violence. Which explains why the marginal phenomena I am focusing upon are now multiplying. In these, neopagan and corrupted Judeo-Christian elements are mixed in such an intricate way that, to unravel them all, a more detailed analysis would be needed.

The process which has denied God first, then man, and finally even the individual, has not destroyed the competitive urge which, on the contrary, is becoming more and more intense. It is this competitive urge that loads us with tremendous and futile burdens, and we vainly try to shake them off by blaming the old scapegoats of the modernists and postmodernists.

But here comes good news at long last. The whole problem, I hear, is about to be solved in the most modern and technological fashion. Some researchers have just developed a truly miraculous food that will be "very tasty," they claim, but not nourishing at all: it will be evacuated in its entirety. Very soon, therefore, we will be able to enjoy a perpetual binge and eat twenty-four hours a day without even having to vomit! We will still have to spend a certain amount of time in the bathroom, I suppose, but not for some abnormal reason; everything will be perfectly normal and legitimate. This is most comforting. This great discovery may well be the final victory of modern science over all our false metaphysical superstitions.

An Anthropological Parallel: The Potlatch

Our thinness hysteria is unique, no doubt, because it is inseparable from our unique brand of radical and radically self-defeating "individualism," but some features of our current behavior are duplicated in other cultures, for instance in the famous potlatch of the American Northwest. The great American social critic Thorstein Veblen was already aware of this fact, and in his *Theory of the Leisure Class* he discusses the potlatch within the context of what he calls conspicuous consumption.

Showing off one's wealth has always seemed important to the nouveau riche type everywhere, and in our world there have never been as many nouveaux riches as in America. Being immigrants, or children of immigrants, these people could not pretend they came from old and prestigious families; money was the sole instrument of their snobbery.

When the wealthy become accustomed to their own wealth, straight conspicuous consumption loses its appeal, and the nouveaux riches turn into *anciens riches*. They perceive this change as the *summum* of cultural refinement, and they do their best to make it as conspicuous as the former consumption. They invent a conspicuous non-consumption, therefore, superficially discontinuous with the attitude it supersedes but, at a deeper level, a mimetic escalation of the same process.

In our society conspicuous non-consumption is present in many areas, in clothes for instance. The torn blue jeans, the ill fitting jacket, the baggy pants, the refusal to dress up, are forms of conspicuous non-consumption. The politically correct reading of this phenomenon is that the rich young people regard their own superior buying power with a feeling of guilt, and they desire, if not to be poor, at least to look poor. This interpretation is too idealistic. The real purpose is a calculated indifference to clothes, an ostentatious rejection of ostentation. The message is: "I am beyond a certain type of consumption. I cultivate more esoteric pleasures than the crowd." To abstain voluntarily from something, no matter what, is the ultimate demonstration that one is superior to that something and to those who covet it.

The wealthier we are, the more precious the objects must be for which we deign to compete. Very rich people no longer compare themselves through the mediation of clothes, automobiles, or even houses. The more wealthy we are, in other words, the less grossly materialistic we can afford to be in a hierarchy of competitive games that become more and more rarefied as the escalation continues. Ultimately this process may turn into a complete rejection of competition, which is not always but may be the most intense competition of all.

In order to understand this better, we only have to think of the potlatch which really illustrates not the straight type of conspicuous consumption but the inverted type. Among the Kwakiutl and other Northwestern Indian tribes, great chiefs used to demonstrate their superiority by giving away their most precious possessions to their competitors, the other great chiefs. They all tried to outdo one another in their contempt for wealth. The winner was the one who gave up the most and received the least. This strange game was institutionalized, and it resulted in the destruction of the goods which the two groups, in principle, were trying to give to each other, just as most human groups do in all kinds of ritual exchange.

Vast quantities of wealth were thus squandered in competitive displays of indifference to wealth, the real purpose of which was prestige. There can be rivalries of renunciation rather than acquisition, of deprivation rather than of enjoyment.

At one time, the Canadian authorities made the potlatch

illegal, and we can well understand why. They realized that this search for collective prestige ultimately benefited the big chiefs only and had a negative impact on the vast majority of the people. It is always dangerous for a community to place negative forms of prestige ahead of the positive which do not yet contradict the real needs of human beings.

Even in our society, there can be a competitive aspect to gift giving which, in the potlatch, becomes exacerbated almost beyond recognition. The normal purpose of exchanging gifts, in all societies, is to prevent mimetic rivalries from getting out of hand. The spirit of rivalry is so powerful, however, that it can transform from the inside even institutions that exist only for the purpose of preventing it. The potlatch testifies to the formidable stubbornness of mimetic rivalry. It may be defined as a frozen slice of mimetic crisis that becomes ritualized and finally plays a role, but at great cost, in the control and attenuation of the competitive fever.

In any society, competition can assume paradoxical forms because it can contaminate the activities most alien to it in principle, especially the gift. In the potlatch, as well as in our world, the drive toward less and less can substitute for the drive toward more and more and ultimately mean the same thing.

Unnatural thinness may well be to our society what a great destruction of blankets and furs was among Northwest Indians, with this difference, however, that in the potlatch everything is sacrificed to the pride of the group, which was embodied in the big chief whereas, in the modern world, we compete as individuals, against all other individuals. The community is nothing and the individual is everything. We have identified the enemy and he is us. Every individual ends up with his own personalized equivalent of the potlatch madness.

A Brief History of Competitive Dieting

The anthropological key opens the antechamber of competitive dieting, but the inner sanctum remains closed. Since mimetic phenomena always tend to escalate, they must have a beginning, a development, and finally an end, which is not yet in sight in the case of our eating disorders . . . Mimetic phenomena have their own specific temporality or historicity, and they must be read in a historical as well as in an anthropological key.

The history of the rage for slenderness can be reconstituted, at least in part. It all began, as it should, as in a fairy tale, with some beautiful and prestigious women in very high places. The most important of these mimetic models was Elizabeth of Austria, the wife of Emperor Franz Joseph, better known as Sisi. She presented herself as a "new woman."

Being unhappy as a wife and mother she sought an *identity* of her own, away from ceremonial obligations. She tried to find it in a special body culture which made her into the prototype of the modern "advanced" woman (see Vandereycken and van Deth).

Sisi's life pattern was typically anorexic; she insisted on a rigid low-calorie diet, and she dedicated herself to gymnastics and various sports in a manner prophetic of our own time. Together with the wife of Napoleon III, Empress Eugenie of France, another famous beauty, Sisi put an end to the crinoline that imprisoned the lower part of a woman's body. At some encounter of their two imperial husbands, these great ladies retired to a private room for the purpose, we are told, of comparing their respective waistlines. This incident suggests some kind of incipient competition between the two, exactly what was needed to start a pattern of mimetic rivalry among the numerous aristocratic ladies who had nothing to do but to look up to Sisi and Eugenie and copy their behavior down to the last detail. The two empresses certainly played a role in the triggering of the mimetic rivalry that has been widening and intensifying ever since. After World War I, the escalation reached the middle class, and after World War II, at least in the opulent West, it spread to all social classes.

We still have princesses, of course, but in keeping with the rest of our civilization, they have gone down one notch or two. The bulimic pattern is more characteristic of them than the heroic anorexia of the "genuinely" quixotic Sisi.

It is interesting to observe that the first clinical descriptions of anorexia were written at the very time when Sisi and Eugenie exerted their greatest influence (Louis-Victor Marcé in 1860, Lasègue and Gull in 1873). This first medical anorexia seems to have been primarily an upper class illness. The Hollywood stars of the thirties look rather plump by our standards, but they seemed elegantly thin in their own time, and by pre–World War I standards they appeared downright skinny. By 1940 the trend was so powerful that the food shortages of WWII did not even slow it down. Since that time, with each passing decade, it has become more extreme. The crisis stage is reached when competition feeds exclusively upon itself, forgetting its initial objects. Anorexic women are not interested in men at all; not unlike these men, they compete among themselves, for the sake of competition itself.

The specialists readily acknowledge the mimetic dimension of eating disorders, but their understanding remains superficial. They are aware that when one case of bulimia becomes known in some college, a few days later, there may be hundreds of cases. But they still conceive imitation in nineteenth-century terms as the purely passive social contagion described by such authors as Tarde, Baldwin, Le Bon, etc. They do not see the competitive dimension, the whole mimetic escalation. They do not see, therefore, that they are dealing with a historical phenomenon.

The rivalry intensifies as the number of imitators increases. The reason for our reluctance to perceive the escalation is that we hate to acknowledge our own mimetic fads as much as we love to acknowledge the *mimesis* of others. All cultures tend to be comical in each other's eyes but never in their own eyes. The same is true of the past in relation to the present.

The spirit of rivalry may triumph in the absence of any specific rival. The whole process is a milder version of Hobbes's "war of all against all." It may also be compared to a series of athletic records that get broken faster and faster as more and more people try to break them.

The constant exaggeration of the collective syndrome is inseparable from its diffusion to larger and larger crowds. Once the mimetic ideal is defined, everybody tries to outdo everybody else in the desired quality, here slenderness, and the weight regarded as most desirable in a young woman is bound to keep going down. All fads and fashions operate dynamically because they operate mimetically. Historians focus exclusively on the supreme phase, just before the collapse. They want to amuse their readers with the foolishness of the past and simultaneously persuade them that their own superior rationality protects our world from similar excesses.

The anorexic ideal of radical emaciation affects more and more areas of human activity. Our professional judgments are often distorted by it. Overweight people complain, no doubt rightly, that they are the object of social and economic discrimination.

Shakespeare's Julius Caesar is suspicious of Cassius's thinness. He detects in it the envy and resentment that, indeed, characterize this personage. Nowadays it is fatness that we distrust. This about-face, however, may not be quite what it seems. What has changed is not our deeper feelings but the culture in which we live, which has become a culture of distrust and, not without reason perhaps, we regard thin people as more able to cope with it than fat ones.

## Our Anorexic Distortion of the Past

In order not to see what is going on, we manage to fool ourselves regarding the past, leaning upon various half-truths or downright lies which, like all propagandists, we keep repeating *ad nauseam*. One of these consists in attributing to the entire European past an inordinate predilection for fat women, rooted, we claim, in an obsession with food resulting from the state of semi-starvation which was normal in those days.

Both historically and esthetically, this theory is illiterate. In preindustrial Europe, more than 80% of the people were living on those small independent units of food production that were called farms. Even if they had wanted to, the most tyrannical rulers and the most unjust landlords would have found it extremely dangerous to starve their own farmers. They were not stupid enough to forget that they depended on these people for the production of their own food.

During their occupation of Western Europe, the Nazis starved city dwellers quite efficiently, but the farmers and all the people with farm connections never starved. The only leaders who succeeded in creating huge famines were Stalin and Mao who, in obeisance to their communist dogma, destroyed independent farming and killed more people than all medieval famines combined.

The idea that semi-starvation was a more or less permanent feature of life in pre-industrial Europe is a gross falsification of the evidence and, even if food shortages had been as common as now claimed, it is most doubtful that they would have influenced the conception of feminine beauty held by painters and sculptors. In these days, aesthetic fashions did not originate with the lower classes but with people too closely associated to the ruling circles not to share in their privileges, at least as far as food was concerned. Even in times of famine, artists were certainly among the last to go hungry. There is nothing to suggest that they dreamed about food half as much as we do.

The fatness imperative we clamp upon the past is a crude projection of our own obsession with food, an obvious maneuver to deny our own singularity. Our innumerable cookbooks and gourmet magazines, our false jolliness in matters alimentary, our endless cooking shows and our perpetual celebration of good eating, demonstrate that the most food obsessed culture in Western history is our own. This obsession is a well-known symptom of anorexia.

Judging from the history of painting, there never was anything in the past remotely similar to our preoccupation with how much a woman should weigh, or with the possible cellulite deposits on the thighs of the women painted by such people as Rembrandt and Rubens!

Before our century, there were variations of taste, no doubt, in schools of painting as well as in individual painters, but they cannot be reduced to any single factor. In Flemish painting, women seem fatter, as a rule, than in Italian painting, but exceptions abound. Vermeer paints his female figures thinner than Titian and Tintoretto. Must we assume that he was the best fed of the three?

With the possible exception of the huge breasts, bellies, and derrières of prehistorical Venuses, the fatness imperative in the history of art seems to be one of the lesser canards in the vast constellation of myths generated by our passion for unnatural thinness. In order not to perceive how exceptional we are, we treat the exception—ourselves—as if it were the rule, and the rule—everybody else—as the exception. We piously deplore "ethnocentric fallacies" that dissolved long ago in the massive uniformity of our age, but we never notice the one fallacy that obviously afflicts us all, the "modernocentric" fallacy.

The tendency to mistake ourselves for the umbilic of the

universe and judge everything from our twisted standpoint is visible in all areas of our culture. One of the real howlers is the current interpretation of religious asceticism as "an early form of anorexia." It should be paired with the revealing justification some of our anthropologists provide for infanticide in archaic culture: "an early means of population control."

There is such a thing as genuine religious asceticism, and great works testify to its existence in all periods of our history. When sanctity is officially valued, however, the desire not to be a saint but to be *regarded* as one is bound to become a goal of mimetic rivalry. Just as other types of human behavior, religious asceticism can be competitive. But the churches were on guard against such distortions which, at the most, involved a few hundred people, not millions like our current eating disorders. We hate our Christian past so much that we accuse it simultaneously of encouraging anorexia and of "discouraging the great mystics." We never give it the benefit of the doubt and envisage the possibility that it might have encouraged mysticism while discouraging anorexia.

Those who despise the past never seem to suspect that far worse excesses are now going on right under their noses, on a scale unprecedented, no doubt, since the beginning of human history. In the Middle Ages, the possibility of false asceticism was always acknowledged, at least by intelligent observers, whereas our eating disorders are discussed exclusively in medical terms, as if they had nothing to do with the culture at large and its recent evolution.

The problem with our "scientific" observers is that they worship the same idols as their patients. They may be compulsory dieters themselves, or would-be dieters. Few people want to be saints nowadays, but everybody is trying to lose weight.

With the end of the last remaining religious prohibitions a most benign and marvelous ritual came to an end, the family meal, a major roadblock, no doubt, on the path to vomiting bulimia. Industrial food is unquestionably easier to vomit than your mother's cooking. The deregulation of meals has had effects similar to the deregulation of air travel. The whole process has become inexpensive, no doubt, but bumpy, chaotic, unreliable, and supremely uncomfortable. More and more people eat alone, at irregular times, and they hurriedly consume vast quantities of junk food. It is interesting that, in their famous binges, bulimic patients accentuate these typical features to the point of caricature. They show a marked preference for cheap pastry and all the mushy and greasy horrors produced by our food industry, which they consume in great haste. This haste is the only point of resemblance with the Passover meal.

In the "developed" world, the forces that pull us in the direction of consumption are just as powerful as the forces that pull us in the direction of fasting. On the side of excessive consumption, there is the cheapness of food, its ready availability, the enormous advertising pressure and also, last but not least, the collapse of all religious and ethical restraints.

Our entire culture looks more and more like a permanent conspiracy to prevent us from reaching the goals it perversely assigns to us. No wonder if we are also the culture from which many people want to drop out, as a result of sheer exhaustion, and also, perhaps, of a peculiar kind of boredom. In the United States, obesity is even more on the rise than extreme slenderness, especially in those geographical areas and social classes that are less "with it" than the rest of us. One cannot help feeling sympathy for all these drop-outs. In all aspects of life, the oscillation between all and nothing, which is the fruit of hysterical competition, is more and more visible. Even in Europe, where formerly, all classes still lived in all neighborhoods, the cities are dividing between dilapidated sections and the sanitized areas with the enormous houses and the manicured lawns.

## The Culture of Anorexia

The mimetic escalations that culminate in anorexia/bulimia are at work in all areas of our culture. The most revealing one, no doubt, is that of "high culture," which was the first, probably, to be contaminated with "anorexic" tendencies long before losing weight became the universal obsession.

In all arts, beginning with painting, and continuing with music, architecture, literature, and philosophy, the ideal of radicalism and revolution have long been dominant. What these labels concretely imply is the escalation of a competitive game, which invariably consists in discarding one by one all traditional principles and practices of every art. The late comers being still dedicated to the same anti-mimetic principles as their predecessors, they must paradoxically imitate them by doing away with whatever has not yet been discarded by the previous waves of radicalism. With each generation, a new batch of iconoclasts boast that they are the sole genuine revolutionists, but they all really imitate one another, and the more they try, the less they can get away from imitation. There have been temporary interruptions of these dynamics, no doubt, and even brief reversals, in the overall history of modernism, but the main thrust is undeniable, and it has become so obvious that the systemics of revolution have finally broken down or are in the process of breaking down.

In painting, the realistic rendition of light and shadow was first discarded, and then more and more essential elements, traditional perspective, and finally all recognizable shape, and color itself. In architecture and furniture the evolution was the same. In poetry, rhyming was abandoned, and then all metrical aspects. The word 'minimalism' now designates only one particular school, but it fits nicely the whole dynamics of modernism. In poetry, in the novel, in drama, and all other genres of writing, this process keeps repeating itself. First, all realistic context is eliminated, then the plot, then the characters; finally the sentences lose their coherence and even the words themselves, which may be replaced by a significant or, better still, an incoherent jumble of letters.

All schools, of course, do not do away with the same things at the same time, and local differences have often resulted in brilliant if short-lived creative outbursts. Ultimately, however, everybody and everything tends towards the same absolute nothing which is now triumphant in all fields of esthetic endeavor. More and more critics are beginning to face up to the fact that vigorous novelty is drying up. Modern art is over, and its end was certainly hastened, if not entirely caused, by the more and more anorexic temper of our century.

Not only is our literature suffused with the spirit of anorexia and bulimia but these conditions are now the subject of literary works such as Valérie Rodrigue, *La peau à l'envers* or Stephanie Grant, *The Passion of Alice*. Someday, no doubt, there will be an MLA section dedicated to this appetizing new field. But I doubt that anyone will soon equal "A Hunger Artist" of Franz Kafka. In order to understand this work, one must be aware that in the nineteenth and early twentieth century so-called "living skeletons" and "fasting artists" were exhibited for a price at fairs and circuses. They all boasted that they had broken all previous records of emaciation. They were a cross between freaks and sporting champions.

Kafka's story is an allegory of our entire culture. The author obviously sees his own art as representative of the negative, gnostic, and egotistical tendencies present in our world. All this was brilliantly analyzed by Claude Vigée, the French poet and essayist in a book entitled *Les artistes de la faim*.

There are now more literal readings. There are reasons to believe that Kafka himself had anorexic tendencies. To a psychiatrist such as Gerd Schütze, his story represents "the essence, tragedy and desire of anorexics in a way only an insider is able to." This view does not contradict but completes the literary and cultural interpretation of Vigée. Certain trends were visibly at work in our culture long before they influenced our alimentation, and the current prominence of physical anorexia and its bulimic variations must be regarded as an essential moment in the tragic and grotesque revelation of what is happening to us, which is much more significant than an epidemic that would hit us at random, or a bizarre cultural fad unconnected with the general evolution of our society.

In the conclusion of Kafka's story, the crowds lose interest in the *Hungerkünstler* who is finally swept out of his cage and replaced not by someone in the same line of work but by a muscular and menacing panther. This ending is often regarded, rather convincingly in my view, as prophetic of the Nazi era.

The story as a whole, however, and its autobiographical echoes, are prophetic of a later era, our own, in which the metaphor is turning into a massive existential fact, resulting in an uncanny and enlightening reversal of the conventional relationship between metaphor and reality. When our relativists maintain that only metaphors exist, they do not realize how right they are. They underestimate the power of certain metaphors to become terrifyingly real.

All this seems now behind us, however, since our postmodern culture has rejected the principle of novelty at any price. The fetish of innovation has been replaced by chaotic eclecticism. But far from rehabilitating the pious and patient imitation of the classics, postmodernism insolently and indolently appropriates just about anything in the past, for no discernible purpose, and certainly not for providing us with the solid nourishment we so desperately need. The new school implicitly denies all permanent value to the past from which it borrows. It quickly regurgitates whatever it indiscriminately ingurgitates and the temptation is great for me to reduce the whole affair to the esthetic equivalent not of anorexia this time, but of our most up-to-date syndrome, bulimia nervosa. Like our princesses, our intellectuals and artists are reaching the bulimic stage of modernity.

Whatever the case may be, the escalation is not really over and we should prepare ourselves for even bigger and better things. If our ancestors could see the gesticulating cadavers of contemporary fashion magazines they would probably interpret them as a *memento mori,* a reminder of death, equivalent, perhaps, to the *danses macabres* on the walls of late medieval churches. If we could tell them that, to us, these disarticulated skeletons signify pleasure, happiness, luxury, success, they would probably flee in a panic, thinking that we are possessed by a particularly nasty devil.

## Note

This text was delivered as a lecture at a COV&R conference in 1995 and published in the journal *Contagion* in 1996.

## Works Cited

Bruch, Hilde. 1973. *Eating Disorders.* New York: Basic Books.

Grant, Stephanie. 1995. *The Passion of Alice.* Boston: Houghton Mifflin.

Kafka, Franz. 1979. "A Hunger Artist." In *The Basic Kafka.* New York: Washington Square Pen Books, 80–90.

Rodrigue, Valérie. 1989. *La peau à l'envers: le roman vrai d'une boulimique.* Paris: Robert Laffont.

Russell, G.M.F. 1979. "Bulimia Nervosa: An Ominous Variant of Anorexia Nervosa." *Psychological Medicine* 9: 429–48.

Schütze, Gerd. 1980. *Anorexia Nervosa.* Bern, Stuttgart and Vienna: H. Huber.

Vandereycken, Walter, and Ron van Deth. 1994. *From Fasting*

*Saints to Anorexic Girls.* New York: New York University Press.

Veblen, Thorstein. 1899. *Theory of the Leisure Class.* New York: Macmillan.

Vigée, Claude. 1960. *Les artistes de la faim.* Paris: Calmann-Lévy.

# A Conversation with René Girard

*With Mark R. Anspach and Laurence Tacou*

**Mark Anspach:** René Girard, could you begin by telling us something about the origin of the text published here? What led you to reflect upon a subject like anorexia?

**René Girard:** My interest in the subject goes all the way back to my childhood. There were cases of anorexia—not very severe but real enough—in my own family, in particular a young cousin whom I talk about in the text. Consequently, when I read Claude Vigée's book *Les artistes de la faim* (1960), it brought back memories. Later, when I decided to write on the subject myself, I took that book as my starting point, since I knew Vigée.

**M.A.:** How did you get to know him?

**R.G.:** When he was teaching in America, at Brandeis, I was a young professor at Bryn Mawr, not so far away. We must have become acquainted at a meeting of the Modern Language Association. He was the first friend I made in academia. We looked each other up in France, as well, and we continued to exchange our respective books. There was a great bond of sympathy between us. He was an Alsatian Jew who had immigrated to the United States as I had. He was the colleague to whom I felt the closest.

**M.A.:** Were there any theoretical affinities between you?

**R.G.:** Not really, but at that time I was less of a monomaniac! Still, when I wrote my text on anorexia, it was the contagious, mimetic side of the phenomenon that caught my attention. Vigée hadn't made any forays into contemporary sociology, but in the 1990s, there was an acute consciousness of the problem in American society. There were even lawsuits brought against women's fashion media or designers of *haute couture*. I did a lot of research on the subject. And I also had a kind of informant on campus, a male student who had a good understanding of mimetic theory. He shared with me his observations about other boys at Stanford, about the pressure that worked in favor of anorexia . . .

**M.A.:** What form did this pressure take? Did young people talk about their weight? Make comparisons?

**R.G.:** They made comparisons without even having to talk about it; they knew this preoccupation existed and dominated many aspects of student culture at the time.

**Laurence Tacou:** Anorexia has always been a feminine scourge. Was it really anorexia afflicting boys this time, or were they simply going on a diet to avoid becoming fat?

**R.G.:** These things are very difficult to distinguish. It's true there has never been this kind of dieting among boys in the past. For that reason, many of these students considered this new development to be a masculine extension of the anorexic phenomenon, interpreted as an urge to be thin. It is something very visual, tied to the gaze of the Other. Of course, my informant was well-versed in the theory, so he wasn't a totally impartial witness.

**M.A.:** Did he go on a diet himself?

**R.G.:** He told me that he was in danger of doing so, but his awareness of the collective and social character of the problem held him back. He didn't want to cave in to the pressure; he felt victimized by a social phenomenon that was out of his control.

**M.A.:** It sounds as if he found a remedy of sorts in mimetic theory itself…

**R.G.:** In his case, the knowledge he had of it was a help to him.

**L.T.:** Yet the traditional norms of masculine fashion never glorified the image of the skinny fellow. On the contrary, a man was supposed to be virile; even young ephebes were not thin and frail as a rule; whereas, with girls, there is this image of the anemic young woman, pale…

**R.G.:** Emaciated … The truth is that I did not persevere in my study of the phenomenon, and I don't know to what extent it has progressed among boys. My old informant from Stanford has gone off to teach in a Wisconsin high school. He told me he has observed the same tendencies at work in that school, but without giving many details.

**M.A.:** In fact, it seems there has been a radical change in the type of physique considered desirable among male models. Tan and muscular young men have found themselves shunted aside in favor of pale and skinny boys. The *New York Times* devoted an article to the subject in 2008. The most sought-after models of the moment were not simply thin, but downright emaciated, with spindly arms and concave chests. According to the *Times,* this new trend began around the year 2000 with clothes produced by the stylist Hedi Slimane for Dior Homme.[1] In an advertising campaign for Dior, one could see a male model with a body mass index of 18, which is just short of anorexia.[2]

**L.T.:** It does look like there is growing undifferentiation between men and women.

**R.G.:** The difference between the sexes counts for less and less.

**M.A.:** The new male models are unabashedly effeminate. Some of the boys in these photos are so delicate and sylphlike, so blissfully lacking in strength and vigor, that they appear incapable of undertaking the slightest effort or least bit of work, suggesting that someone else would have to look after their needs. The maintenance of idle creatures unfit for gainful employment is another form of conspicuous consumption described by Thorstein Veblen in *The Theory of the Leisure Class* (1899). In Veblen's time, and up until quite recently, it was the man who went about with a decorative woman on his arm, a trophy wife. Now there is a turnabout, with actresses or female singers showing off their trophy husbands.

**R.G.:** You mean [Nicolas] Sarkozy is Carla Bruni's trophy husband? (*laughter*) She is a more important personage than he is!

**M.A.:** She is surely more important in their own eyes . . . But all the same, she is quite thin. It's no coincidence that she is a model. Speaking of which, she has been appearing in an advertising campaign for a car where she says something like, "Oh, this is just the first thing I found in the garage." . . . It's a good example of what you call the strategy of indifference.

**R.G.:** Like the new pair of blue jeans that is made to look worn and faded before it is sold. There is nothing worse than letting others see that you want to impress them. The same idea is already present in Shakespeare. Take the example of Beatrice and Benedick in *Much Ado About Nothing*. The first to tell the other "I love you" will lose. It reminds me of those bicycle races where it pays not to take the lead too early.

**M.A.:** By letting the other guy get in front, you give yourself a model to emulate while at the same time not letting him see you. The objective is to win without sticking your neck out and making your desire visible. The same strategy underpins minimalist literature, where authors hide their desire to impress behind a mask of indifference. Displaying indifference is itself a way to impress, a putative proof of superiority. I am thinking of the studied neutrality of the narration in *The Stranger*, which you analyze as a stylistic trick through which a young, still unknown Albert Camus concealed his desire to win readers.[3]

**L.T.:** There was a time when one was supposed to display indifference toward food. Polite ladies would eat something at home before going out to dinner, in order not to look gluttonous. Now there is an American television series, *Desperate Housewives*, in which five women—every one of them thin as a rail—spend their time baking and eating cakes … Anorexia is out of favor; you still have to be skinny but not stop eating.

**R.G.:** Bulimia operates on the same principle. Bulimia is a very American, very practical solution to the problem. One can eat, stuff oneself, then get rid of the food. It's the height of technical progress.

**L.T.:** But how does one explain the appeal of the ultra-thin woman—for example Kate Moss, this very famous model who is considered extremely beautiful and sexy despite having hollow cheeks and a rather cadaverous appearance?

**R.G.:** This phenomenon struck me for the first time in a department store one day. On the torso of a mannequin wearing a swimsuit, I noticed that all the ribs were showing. The effect was quite sinister, but it was intentional, which gives one pause. That was about fifteen years ago. What's strange is that these fashions seem to go on forever; they must therefore have a deeper significance. Change is often thought to be the essence of fashion, yet here there is no change; things have been moving in the same direction for more than a hundred years. I believe I cite the wife of the last emperor of Austria, Sissi, and Eugénie, the wife of Napoleon III, who measured each other's waists when they met at some international get-together.

**L.T.:** At the same time, the criteria of beauty have continued to evolve. For example, Marilyn Monroe and Ava Gardner were not at all tall and willowy. They were rather petite and on the plump side, yet they were considered great beauties.

**R.G.:** In fact, that is undoubtedly the physical type men prefer. But women's fashion has become an exclusively feminine affair, an arena for rivalries among women, where there is not necessarily any place for the man.

**L.T.:** What do you think about "fashion victims," these women who are completely wrapped up in a mad obsession with fashion and cannot imagine any other mode of existence?

**R.G.:** Like all obsessive desires—the desire for wealth, the desire for power—it is a passion born of rivalry. These women want to be admired by others. They want to be at the center of the world, and they will go to extraordinary lengths to outdo everyone else. But it is more than an individual quirk; the existence of fashion victims is no doubt the sign of a social crisis. It is a sign of the times. Is there any evidence for something similar in the past? No examples come to mind...

**L.T.:** Whatever examples we might find, it was never a mass phenomenon. In the past, fashion was reserved for the elite; today, it reaches the whole population.

**R.G.:** The phenomenon has been completely democratized. In the era of Sissi and Eugénie, it concerned the highest social classes. It would no doubt have been possible to observe class distinctions based on women's weight. The average weight of women from the social elite would have been lower. The glorification of the very thin woman as an esthetic ideal begins with Art Nouveau. But before about 1920, this tendency to slimness is limited to the aristocracy; then the phenomenon spreads as it descends the social ladder. "*Avoir la ligne*" [to have a slim figure] is an expression that was already in use when I was a small child, but not at the bottom of the ladder. Today, all that has been democratized, leaving aside those who are out of the race because they really refuse to participate in it.

**M.A.:** Poor women are out of the race because they cannot eat right and they become obese.

**R.G.:** In the United States, poor women are fatter than others because they eat fattening food, and also because they do not stint themselves. The two factors converge.

**M.A.:** According to recent statistics, more than half the adults in the world—and almost two thirds of the men—are overweight or obese.[4] People seem to be either too fat or too thin. Curiously, it is those in the middle or "normal" range who are in short supply.

**R.G.:** That may be an exaggeration, but compared to the past, it is certainly the trend.

**L.T.:** There is even a tendency to be too thin and too fat all at once, if you think about silicone-enlarged breasts, plumped-up lips . . .

**M.A.:** Women are being pulled in opposite directions by two contradictory ideals, slenderness and voluptuousness. They cannot conform to both simultaneously.

**R.G.:** It makes one think of the bodies of certain insects that are separated into segments joined by a thread at the abdomen. There is something insect-like in such a physique.

**M.A.:** One sees giant insects in science fiction movies; they are a kind of *monster*. Isn't the appearance of monsters a charac-teristic symptom of a crisis of undifferentiation? American cinema has been crawling with monsters since at least the 1950s. The new development is the advent of female stars with monstrous physiques.

**L.T.:** How should we interpret this body mania that is reaching such extremes? Women today seem to be completely obsessed with their bodies.

**R.G.:** It's linked to the contemporary aesthetic that makes the individual the be-all and end-all, excluding social values of any kind, especially religious ones. It is the principal mani-festation of this phenomenon.

**M.A.:** Do you mean to say that amidst a generalized absence of values, of models of what to do with one's life, people fall back on their bodies? Has the body become the last bastion of the self?

**R.G.:** I think so. Our society is completely materialistic; it is very difficult to find new values.

**L.T.:** Not only is there a lack of values, there is also a lack of *rituals.* Isn't anorexia among adolescents tied to the fact that we live in societies that are entirely "de-ritualized," where there is no longer any recognized passage to adulthood? Young people impose on themselves a kind of initiation rite, obviously copied from a model. They want to surpass their limits by fasting. In the old days there was religion: ritual fasts, Lent, things that hardly exist anymore now. For adolescent girls, isn't there a desire for purity that manifests itself in these fasts?

**R.G.:** Given my preoccupations, I put the emphasis on rivalry. But all of the elements you mention exist, of course; they may be present to begin with or can quite easily be superimposed. The people involved may very well not see their rivalrous motives and be dominated by them without perceiving them. The strange thing is that medieval convents were much more aware of the danger than we are in the modern world.

Handbooks of asceticism took it into account. In the Middle Ages, there was competitive fasting among persons who wanted to earn a reputation as ascetics. There was a positive goal, a veritable ambition to attain dominance, analogous but not identical to modern anorexia, which is linked to the gaze, to the universe of photography. Before, it was a will to power that expressed itself in the desire to be more ascetic than one's neighbor, to be more capable of resisting hunger. With anorexics, hunger is totally dominated; it seems to me to be something that is more centered on the Self. The Other still plays a vital role, but that role is in some way mediated by many external factors. In a convent, where two sisters are in a struggle for dominance, the Other intervenes in a way that is simpler and more direct.

**M.A.:** A convent is not an ordinary place. It is a milieu characterized by a significant degree of undifferentiation. The nuns dress in identical fashion while veiling their hair and body; they follow the same daily routine. They are committed to living together day after day inside the same closed space. If they wanted to gain distinction within such a constrictive framework, competing for ascetic status would be one of the only ways to do so.

**R.G.:** That's right, the point of departure is different, but the tendency to rivalry is always the heart of the matter. And once rivalry is unleashed, there are no longer any limits.

**M.A.:** At first sight, modern society has little in common with a convent, but paradoxical resemblances may exist between the two. In a convent or monastery, everyone is the same sex; in our society, the difference between the sexes is fading, which in a sense comes out to the same thing. The difference between generations is also fading, with adults striving to "stay young" while young people precociously adopt "adult" behaviors. The most basic anthropological categories are in crisis. Doesn't such a context of growing undifferentiation facilitate the explosion of rivalries for objects as frivolous as thinness—rivalries that no cultural guardrail is able to contain, given the decline of traditional religious rituals invoked by Laurence Tacou?

**R.G.:** The modern world abolishes religion, but it produces new rites that are much more onerous and formidable than those of the past—rites that hark back to archaic religious forms in a manner still to be defined.

**M.A.:** Ordeals that test the body, such as the quest for extreme leanness, but also piercings, tattoos . . . ?

**R.G.:** Yes, but the essential is always the Other—an Other who is anyone at all, the incarnation of an impregnable totality, present everywhere and nowhere—that one stubbornly hopes to seduce. It is the Other as insurmountable obstacle. That quickly becomes submission to a purely metaphysical imperative. If you do not have a real religion, you end up with a more dreadful one . . .

**M.A.:** One of the great prophets of the dreadful religion that springs up after religion is Franz Kafka, whose "Hunger Artist" you discuss in your text. Kafka made a revealing comparison between Balzac and himself: "Balzac had a walking-stick on which was inscribed the motto: *I crush every obstacle;* my own personal motto is: *Every obstacle crushes me.*"

**R.G.:** That testifies clearly to a change of eras. Balzac could still express the conquering attitude of naïve modernism. But once we get to Kafka, things become more twisted; people begin to tell themselves that a crushable obstacle can't be an obstacle worthy of the name. For Kafka, the last obstacle that remains is precisely that Other who is everywhere and nowhere. It is the omnipresent and anonymous mimetic model.

**L.T.:** There is something that bothers me slightly in this idea of an omnipresent mimetic model. When all is said and done, you always succeed in finding mimetic models everywhere. Doesn't that risk becoming a weakness as much as a strength of your approach? Is there really no limit to the applicability of the mimetic theory?

**R.G.:** Mimetic theory does not apply to all human relations, but even in relationships with those who are closest to us, we must be conscious of the mechanisms it describes. In reality, it is the era in which we live that is like a caricature. Since we all participate in this exaggeration, it becomes paradoxically more difficult to detect than the normality of the past. That is the paradox of my thesis. It may be overstated, but I believe it to be true; and if I persist, it is because I also believe that the truth, today, has lost all verisimilitude.

**L.T.:** Do you think that some people don't like to hear about mimetic theory because it shines a harsh light on things that are ultimately too intimate?

**R.G.:** Most people are perfectly capable of seeing the mimetic theory as a mere social satire that does not implicate them personally. Those with enough sense of humor manage to say, "Yes, I indulge in some of these behaviors; it can happen that I, too, act out of pure imitation." Often, fashions have no meaning; people simply imitate them without reflecting on their significance. The individual becomes a vehicle for a significance that eludes him.

**L.T.:** What about you? Do you think you are susceptible to current fashions or trendy ideas?

**R.G.:** I think that as one gets older, one becomes less so. But certainly I was once. If I hadn't been susceptible myself, I would not have understood the phenomenon. It takes a kind of personal conversion, an acceptance of humiliation, to say to oneself: "I was terribly mimetic on such an occasion; I will try to be less so."

**M.A.:** In an autobiographical text published in the Cahier de l'Herne devoted to you, you describe having suffered in your youth from a particularly acute "mimetic sickness," which manifested itself by a sort of literary snobbery in reverse.[5]

**R.G.:** In ordinary snobbery, the kind described by Proust, one is drawn exclusively to works singled out for attention by prestigious models. My case was still more severe because I was allergic to reading anything suggested by someone else. The most extreme form of mimetic malady is an intransigent anti-mimetic attitude because, although one must not be a slave to other people's opinions, it is impossible to shut oneself off from everything that comes from others. The imitation of positive models is inevitable and even indispensable to creativity. By systematically rejecting any external model, one runs the risk of intellectual sterility.

**L.T.:** Aren't you afraid that the mimetic theory itself could end up being rejected if it becomes *too* fashionable and gains so much popularity as to provoke a backlash?

**R.G.:** In the short run, such fluctuations of opinion as a result of opposing trends are always possible. But in the long run, I believe that a theory will prove lasting if it has a strong footing in reality—I am an unqualified realist in this sense. The mimetic understanding of reality is still at a very early stage. A time will come when all this will seem obvious. There will be a shift from a refusal to see the phenomenon to seeing it everywhere ... But nothing is certain, of course.

**M.A.:** A moment ago, Laurence Tacou asked whether there are any limits to the mimetic interpretation. I would like to raise the same question in the specific context of eating disorders. Many observers recognize the pernicious influence of cultural models that promote an ideal of extreme thinness, but this influence affects all women, while anorexia in the strict sense—the kind that undermines health and can lead to death—remains quite rare. Why, then, does the most severe pathology strike only some women and not the rest? Gérard Apfeldorfer, a psychiatric expert on eating disorders interviewed by the French daily *Libération*, asserts: "Anorexia is not a choice, it's a mental illness. There are psychological predispositions, familial antecedents. In its most widespread form, this disease reflects a narcissistic disorder, not an effort to imitate fashion models."[6]

**R.G.:** I am against this type of explanation in terms of conventional psychology. I do not believe in the existence of narcissism as defined by Freud. We are all self-centered and other-dependent in the same measure; the two go together. We all compare ourselves to others, we all are prone to mimetic rivalry, but not everyone carries this tendency to the point of pathology. Why does anorexia strike some women more than the rest? Individuals are more or less rivalrous; this is just as true where thinness is concerned as in other areas. Anorexic women want to be the champions in their category. It's the same in the world of finance. The only difference is that the desire to be richer than others is not seen as pathological. By contrast, the desire to be thinner, if taken too far, has devastating physical effects that are visible in the body. But once a girl is anorexic and has undertaken to compete in this arena, it is difficult for her to give up before attaining victory—that would mean renouncing the championship. The final result is tragic in the most extreme cases, but that should not make us lose sight of the fact that the obsession with thinness characterizes our entire culture; it is not something that distinguishes these young women from everyone else.

**M.A.:** In her classic study of eating disorders, Hilde Bruch lists some common features in her own clinical observations about 51 anorexic patients and their families. She notes among other things that the patients' fathers were "enormously preoccupied with outer appearances in the physical sense of the word, admiring fitness and beauty."[7]

**R.G.:** And, therefore, thinness! The fathers are important here as representatives of the society at large; they are vectors of transmission for the surrounding culture. When Freud talks about the father and mother, their status remains ambiguous. It is never clear whether parents are important for biological reasons, or because they dominate the life of the child from the start. Freud remains equivocal on this point.

**M.A.:** In fact, Hilde Bruch adds that the preoccupation of the patients' fathers with physical appearance, as well as their desire to see their children "succeed," are doubtless traits shared by many upper-middle-class families, even if these same traits may be found in a more pronounced form in the families of anorexics.

**R.G.:** Anorexia is a phenomenon that appears in an era in which the family is breaking down. To try at all costs to find an explanation for it in the patients' families is to stay locked into a schema that is less and less relevant.

**M.A.:** A leading Italian authority on anorexia, Mara Selvini

Palazzoli, the founder of the Milan school of family therapy, made an observation about the families of anorexics that should interest you all the same. According to her, the patients' parents are caught up in a rivalry to occupy the position of the sacrificial victim . . . [8]

**R.G.:** Psychologists may turn out to be right here or there, in individual cases. But to use these to deny the social nature of a phenomenon that has been growing on all sides for the past 150 years—in my view, that is just a way to hide from ourselves what has become the norm in our society.

**M.A.:** All right, let's get away from the question of families and return one last time to a consideration of the social context. I have already emphasized the fact that the exacerbation of the anorexic phenomenon has occurred in a context of increasing undifferentiation, of undifferentiation between the sexes and between generations. One could speak of a crisis of differences and perhaps even of a "sacrificial crisis" in your sense, meaning a crisis that cannot be resolved by resorting to ritual sacrifices and which, therefore, lends itself to spontaneous, untamed outbreaks of victimage. At the end of your text you compare the images of "gesticulating cadavers" in fashion magazines to the *danses macabres* and *memento mori* of the Middle Ages. I wonder whether we should not interpret in victimary terms the appeal of cadaverous-looking models like Kate Moss.

**L.T.:** In reality, this is a recurrent phenomenon that seems to be associated with adolescence. Something analogous could be witnessed with the "living dead" in the Romantic era; it was the height of chic to be at the point of death.

**M.A.:** More recently, the term "heroin chic" was applied to waifish models with dark circles under the eyes and a junkie's blank stare. Not only does Kate Moss have an emaciated appearance, she is also known for her drug use. When images of her snorting cocaine circulated, the immediate reaction was negative, with advertising campaigns cancelled. But ultimately, the episode gave her career a boost (no pun intended). It would be easy to cite more examples: Britney Spears, Amy Winehouse . . . Of course, there is nothing new about this;

all self-respecting youth idols must flirt with self-destruction in order to burnish their image as doomed divinities, but my impression is that the whole process is turning into a caricature of itself.

**R.G.:** As in the case of thinness, there is a mimetic escalation. The need to commit ever bigger transgressions leads to behaviors that, if they are imitated, prove incompatible with organized society. Social life gets out of whack.

**M.A.:** The first victims of such societal breakdown are the individuals who follow these mimetic fashions to the point of making the supreme sacrifice. I am thinking of young models who collapse on the catwalks, like the 22-year-old Uruguayan woman who died at a fashion show in Spain on August 2, 2006. It is said that she had gone without eating for two weeks, after spending months on a regimen of nothing but lettuce and Diet Coke.[9] These are "fashion victims" in the most literal sense of the term. They give their lives to realize an ideal promoted by the community.

**R.G.:** It's a little like the suicide-terrorist, for those who support his actions—a kind of martyr.

**L.T.:** Martyrs to fashion, as it were . . .

**M.A.:** The comparison might seem bold, but I don't think it is off the mark. It even works both ways because in certain countries, in certain environments—and whatever the religious or political motivations may be—suicide-terrorism has clearly become a fashion craze. Fads are not a uniquely Western phenomenon. It would be a mistake to underestimate the role they play in other cultures. No human society is immune to the power of imitation. In Iraq, for example, after the fall of Saddam Hussein, there was a great vogue for religious extremism that seems already to be abating somewhat. According to a government official in Baghdad, Iraqis embraced religious fervor just as if they had "wanted to put on a new, stylish outfit."[10] In short, suicide-terrorists are martyrs to fashion, too. There are martyrs to fashion everywhere, but it is easier for us to see martyrdom in other cultures and fashion in our own.

**R.G.:** We don't see the martyrdom in our own culture when we look at certain sinister images displayed in fashion magazines, images in which a healthy society would perceive the lineaments of death. It really is something that remains unconscious.

**M.A.:** What about the young women, fashion models or not, who actually do die while trying to conform to these images? If, in going all out to fulfill an ideal promoted by the community, they are led into martyrdom, can we describe them as sacrificial victims? That is the last question I would like to ask you: Should we see this as a sacrifice in the sense of your anthropological theory?

**R.G.:** The imperative for which these women allow themselves to die of hunger comes from the whole society. It is a unanimous imperative. From that point of view, it is indeed organized like a sacrifice. And the fact that it is unconscious demonstrates, rather alarmingly, that there is a kind of return to the archaic in our culture.

# Notes

1. Guy Trebay, "The Vanishing Point," *New York Times,* February 7, 2008.

2. Paola De Carolis, "Viso pallido, corpo emaciato: I ragazzi 'taglia zero,'" *Corriere della Sera,* February 11, 2008.

3. René Girard, "Camus's Stranger Retried," in *"To double business bound": Essays on Literature, Mimesis, and Anthropology* (Baltimore: Johns Hopkins, 1978), 9–35. Stefano Tomelleri, who compares this article to Girard's text on eating disorders, sees in Meursault's conspicuous solipsism and the anorexic's competitive self-destruction two complementary expressions of contemporary nihilism; see Tomelleri's introduction to a collection of essays by Girard published in Italy, *Il risentimento* (Milan: Raffaello Cortina, 1999), 14–16.

4. B. Balkau et al., "A Study of Waist Circumference, Cardiovascular Disease, and Diabetes Mellitus in 168,000 Primary Care Patients in 63 Countries," *Circulation* 116 (October 2007): 1942–1951.

5. René Girard, "Souvenirs d'un jeune Français aux Etats-Unis,"

in *Cahier Girard,* ed. M. R. Anspach (Paris: Editions de l'Herne, 2008), 30.

6. Quoted by Cécile Daumas, "Le corps du délit," *Libération*, September 29, 2006.

7. Hilde Bruch, *Eating Disorders: Obesity, Anorexia Nervosa, and the Person Within* (London: Routledge & Kegan Paul, 1974), 82.

8. Mara Selvini Palazzoli, *L'anoressia mentale: Dalla terapia individuale alla terapia familiare*, revised edition (Milan: Raffaello Cortina, 2006), 220.

9. Daumas, "Le corps du délit."

10. Sabrina Tavernise, "Young Iraqis Are Losing Their Faith in Religion," *New York Times,* March 3, 2008.